Schott Piano Classics

Alexander Reinagle
1756 – 1809

24 Short and Easy Pieces
24 kleine und leichte Spielstücke
24 petites pièces faciles

Intended as the First Lessons for the Pianoforte
Für den ersten Unterricht am Klavier
Pour les premières leçons de piano

opus 1

Herausgegeben von / Edited by / Édité par
Hans-Günter Heumann

ED 22397
ISMN 979-0-001-14958-7

www.schott-music.com

Mainz · London · Berlin · Madrid · New York · Paris · Prague · Tokyo · Toronto
© 2015 SCHOTT MUSIC GmbH & Co. KG, Mainz · Printed in Germany

Inhalt / Contents / Sommaire

Vorwort

Alexander Reinagle wurde 1756 in Portsmouth geboren, allerdings besteht über sein exaktes Geburtsdatum Unklarheit (getauft wurde er am 23. April 1756). Den ersten Unterricht bekam er bei seinem Vater Joseph Reinagle und Raynor Taylor, dem Direktor des königlichen Theaters von Edinburgh. Hier hatte er am 9. April 1770 bereits mit 14 Jahren seinen ersten Auftritt als Cembalist. Reinagle lebte ab 1778 als Cembalolehrer in Glasgow, wo auch seine ersten gedruckten Kompositionen erschienen, wie z. B. sein erstes Opus, die vorliegenden *24 Short and Easy Pieces* (ca. 1780). 1784 lernte er Carl Philipp Emanuel Bach (den berühmtesten Sohn von Johann Sebastian Bach) in Hamburg kennen und blieb mit ihm einige Zeit in brieflichem Kontakt. Zusammen mit seinem Bruder Hugh, einem Cellisten, trat er am 8. Januar 1785 vor der königlichen Familie in Portugal auf. Im selben Jahr wurde er Mitglied der *Royal Society of Musicians* in London. 1786 emigrierte er in die Vereinigten Staaten von Amerika, wo er sich zunächst in New York als Pianist, Violin- und Klavierlehrer betätigte. Noch im selben Jahr übersiedelte er nach Philadelphia. Hier setzte er fast 10 Jahre lang die Tradition der dortigen Stadtkonzerte fort und komponierte seine als *Philadelphia Sonatas* bekannten vier Klaviersonaten. Diese gelten als die ersten in den USA komponierten Klaviersonaten und zeigen großen Einfluss von seinem Idol C. Ph. E. Bach. Reinagle war in Amerika auch als Pädagoge aktiv. Eine seiner Schülerinnen war Nellie Custis, die Stiefenkelin des US-Präsidenten George Washington. Ab 1793 bis 1803 fungierte Reinagle als musikalischer Leiter des *New Theatre* in Philadelphia. Er komponierte hierfür u. a. Ballette und Opern. Außerdem arrangierte und orchestrierte er die Musik zu vielen Aufführungen. Viele seiner Kompositionen gingen im Jahr 1820 bei einem Brand des Theaters verloren. 1803 übersiedelte Reinagle nach Baltimore, wo er ebenfalls musikalischer Leiter des dortigen Theater wurde. Er starb am 21. September 1809 in Baltimore.

Die *24 Short and Easy Pieces* opus 1 schrieb Alexander Reinagle für seine Schüler in England und Schottland. Sie spiegeln sein pädagogisches Interesse wider und sein Talent, einfache, sehr melodische Stücke für den Unterricht zu komponieren. Wie der Untertitel besagt – *intended as the first lessons for the pianoforte or harpsichord* – handelt es sich hier um eine erste Unterweisung für den Klavier- bzw. Cembalounterricht mit Anfängern. Den Stücken geht eine kurze, einseitige Einführung in die Notenschrift voraus (Notenlinien, Zwischenräume, Noten im Violin- und Bassschlüssel über 3 Oktaven, Notenwerte, Vorzeichen). Diese knappe Übersicht endet mit folgendem Hinweis Reinagles:

"In learning the following pieces, play the treble and bass of the first part, separately eight or ten times, then join them together and play them thirty or fourty times, the same with the second part, which if done with care one new piece may be learned every day. N. B. Never leave one piece until you can play it well."

Die ersten Stücke dieser Sammlung beginnen im sogenannten Fünftonraum und erweitern diesen dann durch Spreizen der Finger, Lagenwechsel sowie größere Intervalle und Akkorde. Vor den Stücken – die in C-Dur beginnen und nach und nach Tonarten mit maximal zwei Kreuz- und B-Vorzeichen einführen – sind jeweils die entsprechenden Tonleitern über zwei Oktaven mit anschließender Kadenz zu spielen. Diese reizvollen kleinen progressiv angeordneten Spielstücke sind ideale Artikulations-Studien und für das cantable Spiel sowie für den Vortrag prädestiniert. Sie tragen von Anfang an zur Unabhängigkeit beider Hände bei.

Die vorliegende Ausgabe basiert auf der im Jahr 1821 im Verlag G. E. Blake, Philadelphia erschienenen Fassung, auf dessen Titelbild ein *Tafelklavier* abgebildet ist. Dem Original-Notentext fehlen – wie im 18. Jahrhundert üblich – jegliche musikalische Vortragsbezeichnungen, wie Artikulation, Dynamik, Fingersätze und häufig auch Tempoangaben. Diese wurden in jedem Stück sorgfältig eingetragen und sollen dem Schüler als Hilfestellung bei der Interpretation dieser wunderschönen Miniaturen dienen. Die Stücke eignen sich hervorragend für den Unterricht oder das erste Vorspiel in der Musikschule.

Hans-Günter Heumann

Preface

Alexander Reinagle was born in Portsmouth in 1756, though his exact date of birth is uncertain; he was christened on 23 April 1756. He started lessons with his father Joseph Reinagle and with Raynor Taylor, the director of the Theatre Royal in Edinburgh. There he gave his first public performance on the harpsichord at the age of just fourteen on 9 April 1770. From 1778 Reinagle made his living teaching the harpsichord in Glasgow, where his first printed compositions were also published, including his first opus, these *24 Short and Easy Pieces* (c. 1780). He met Carl Philipp Emanuel Bach, the most famous son of Johann Sebastian Bach, in Hamburg in 1784 and for a while the two men corresponded by letter. With his brother Hugh, a cellist, Alexander Reinagle performed in front of the royal family in Portugal on 8 January 1785. In the same year he became a member of the *Royal Society of Musicians* in London. In 1786 Reinagle emigrated to the United States of America, where he initially worked in New York as a pianist and taught violin and piano. That same year he moved to Philadelphia, where for almost ten years he maintained a tradition of municipal concerts and composed four piano sonatas known as the *Philadelphia Sonatas*. These are considered to be the first piano sonatas composed in the USA and reflect the considerable influence of his idol C.P.E. Bach. In America Reinagle also worked as a teacher: one of his pupils was Nellie Custis, the step-granddaughter of US President George Washington. From 1793 until his death Reinagle was musical director of the New Theatre in Philadelphia, for which he composed ballets and operas, as well as arranging and orchestrating music for various productions. Many of his compositions were lost in a fire at the theatre in 1820. In 1803 Reinagle moved to Baltimore, where he again became musical director of the theatre. Reinagle died in Baltimore on 21 September 1809.

Alexander Reinagle wrote these 24 Short and Easy Pieces opus 1 for his pupils in England and Scotland. They reflect his interest in teaching and his talent for composing simple and tuneful pieces for tuition purposes. As the subheading declares, they were written for beginners, *intended as the first lessons for the pianoforte or harpsichord*. Before the pieces comes a short one-page introduction to the music (staves, intervals, music in treble and bass clefs spanning three octaves, note values, key signatures and accidentals). This brief outline ends with the following advice from Reinagle:

"In learning the following pieces, play the treble and bass of the first part, separately eight or ten times, then join them together and play them thirty or forty times, the same with the second part, which if done with care one new piece may be learned every day. N.B. Never leave one piece until you can play it well."

The first pieces in this collection begin within the five-finger range and then extend it by spreading the fingers, changing positions, reaching across larger intervals and playing chords. The pieces – which begin in C major and gradually introduce keys with a maximum of two sharps or flats – are preceded by corresponding scales spanning two octaves, with a concluding cadence. Presented in order of increasing difficulty, these delightful little pieces are ideal studies in articulation and lyrical playing, as well as being intended for performance. Independent use of the two hands is encouraged from the very beginning.

This edition is based on the publication by G. E. Blake, Philadelphia in 1821, where a square piano is depicted on the title page. The original score omits – as was customary in the 18th Century – any kind of performance markings relating to articulation, dynamics, fingerings and often even tempo indications. These have been carefully added for each piece so as to help students with the interpretation of these lovely miniatures. These pieces are excellent for tuition purposes or for students' first school performances.

Hans-Günter Heumann
English translation Julia Rushworth

Préface

Alexander Reinagle est né à Portsmouth (Angleterre) en 1756 – son baptême est daté du 23 avril mais on ignore sa date de naissance exacte. Son père Joseph, ainsi que Raynor Taylor, directeur du Théâtre royal d'Édimbourg, lui donnent ses premières leçons de musique. C'est dans ce théâtre, le 9 avril 1770, à seulement quatorze ans, qu'il donne son premier concert – au clavecin. À partir de 1778, il vit à Glasgow où il est professeur de clavecin et où paraissent ses premières compositions, notamment son premier opus, les *24 Short and Easy Pieces* reprises ici (vers 1780). En 1784, il fait la connaissance, à Hambourg, de Carl Philipp Emanuel Bach, le plus célèbre fils de Jean-Sébastien, et entretient une correspondance avec lui pendant quelque temps. Le 8 janvier 1785, il se produit avec son frère Hugh, violoncelliste, devant la famille royale du Portugal. La même année, il devient membre de la *Royal Society of Musicians* de Londres. En 1786, il émigre aux États-Unis et s'installe tout d'abord à New York, où il mène une existence de pianiste et de professeur de violon et piano. Dans le courant de l'année, il part pour Philadelphie où il va reprendre la tradition des concerts municipaux qu'il dirigera pendant presque dix ans. Là, il écrit ses quatre sonates dites « de Philadelphie », qui sont considérées comme les premières sonates pour piano composées aux États-Unis et trahissent une grande influence du modèle qu'il adule, C. P. E. Bach. Il continue d'enseigner, l'une de ses élèves étant Nellie Custis, parente du président George Washington. De 1793 à 1803, il est directeur musical du New Theatre de Philadelphie. Pour cette scène, il compose des ballets et des opéras et fait également office d'arrangeur et d'orchestrateur (nombre de ses compositions seront détruites par un incendie du bâtiment en 1820). En 1803, il s'installe à Baltimore, où il devient également directeur musical du théâtre des lieux. Il meurt le 21 septembre 1809 à Baltimore.

C'est pour ses élèves d'Angleterre et d'Écosse qu'Alexander Reinagle a écrit ses *24 Short and Easy Pieces* op. 1. Ce recueil reflète son intérêt pédagogique et son talent pour écrire des pièces simples et mélodiques destinées à l'apprentissage de l'instrument. Comme le souligne le sous-titre – « pour les premières leçons de piano ou de clavecin » –, les vingt-quatre morceaux sont conçus à l'intention des débutants qui font leurs premiers pas au piano ou au clavecin. En exergue figure une introduction où Reinagle explique brièvement la notation musicale (lignes de la portée, interlignes, notes en clé de *sol* et en clé de *fa* sur trois octaves, durée des notes, altérations). Ce rapide aperçu se termine par le conseil suivant du compositeur :

« Pour travailler les pièces suivantes, on jouera la première partie les mains séparées huit ou dix fois, puis les mains ensembles trente ou quarante fois ; même chose avec la deuxième partie. Si ce travail est fait soigneusement, l'élève sera en mesure d'apprendre une nouvelle pièce quotidiennement. N.B. Ne jamais abandonner une pièce tant que l'on n'est pas capable de bien la jouer. »

Les premières pièces commencent par la position de base sur cinq notes puis on écarte les doigts, on change de registre et viennent des intervalles plus grands et des accords. Au départ tout est en en *ut* majeur, puis petit à petit sont introduites des tonalités qui ont au maximum deux dièses ou deux bémols. Avant chaque morceau, l'élève est invité à jouer une gamme de deux octaves dans la tonalité correspondante avec une cadence finale. Classés de manière progressive, ces ravissants petits morceaux sont idéals pour le travail de l'articulation, pour apprendre à chanter les mélodies et à jouer avec musicalité. Dès le départ, ils font travailler l'indépendance des mains.

La présente édition est fondée sur l'édition de 1821, parue chez G. E. Blake, où figure un piano carré sur la page de titre. Le texte musical de cette première édition est dépourvu de toute indication destinée à l'interprète – articulation, nuances, doigtés, ou (la plupart du temps) tempi –, comme c'était habituel au XVIIIe siècle. Nous avons soigneusement ajouté nos indications dans chacune de ces merveilleuses miniatures afin d'aider l'élève à les interpréter correctement. Ces morceaux se prêtent aussi bien à l'apprentissage qu'à la première audition à l'école de musique.

Hans-Günter Heumann
Traduction Daniel Fesquet

24 Short and Easy Pieces

24 kleine und leichte Spielstücke / 24 petites pièces faciles opus 1

1. Minuetto

Alexander Reinagle
1756–1809

2. Minuetto

3. Allegro

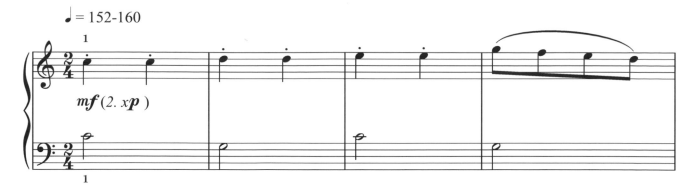

4. Allegro

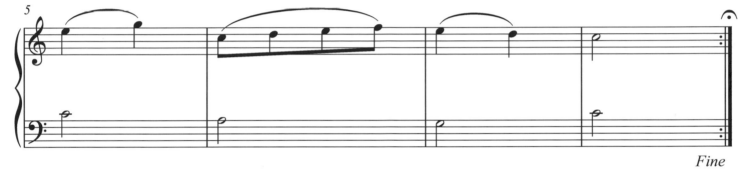

Fine

D.C. al Fine

10

5. Allegretto

6

Allegretto ♩ = 132

12

7

Allegretto ♩ = 138

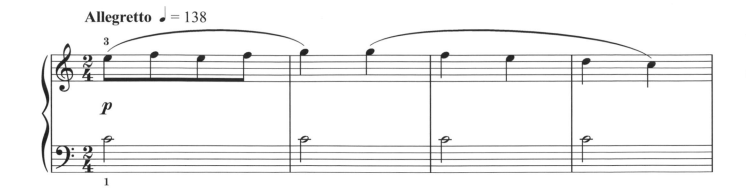

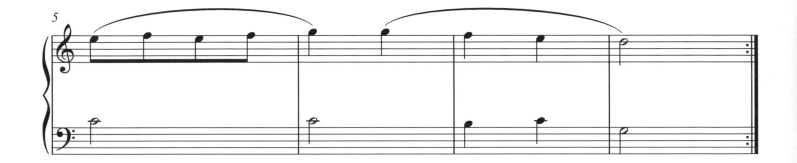

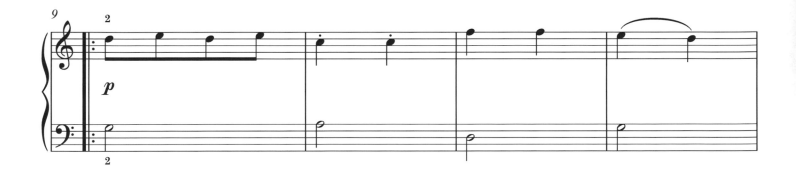

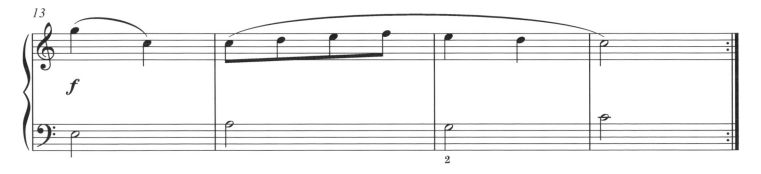

8

Allegretto ♩ = 100

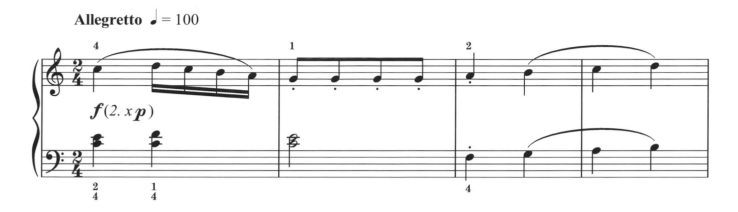

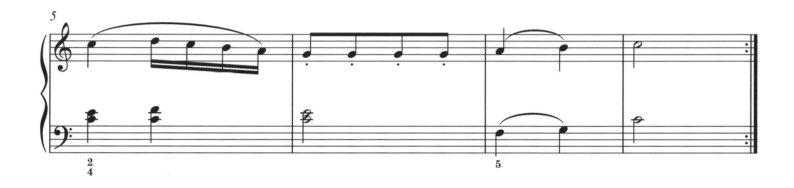

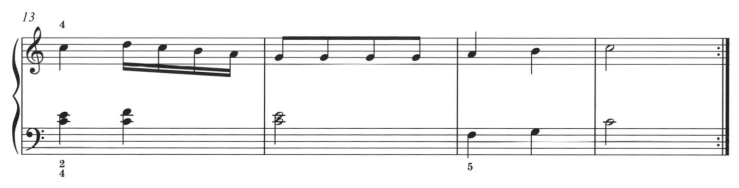

14

9

Allegretto ♩ = 132

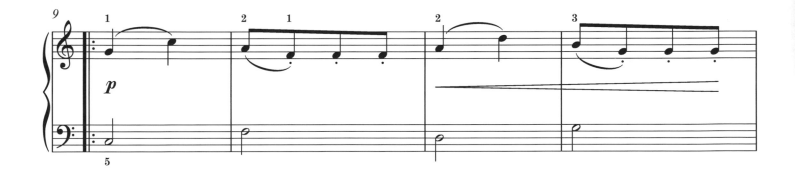

10

Minuetto ♩ = 132-138

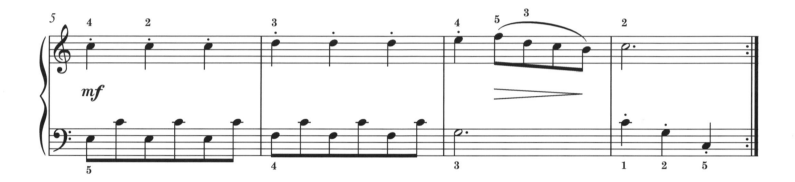

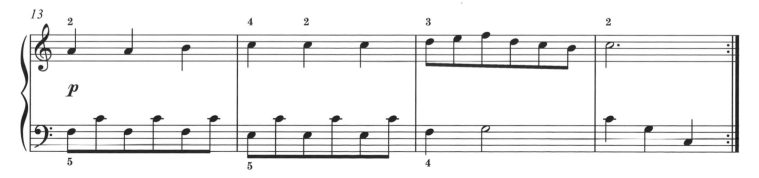

11

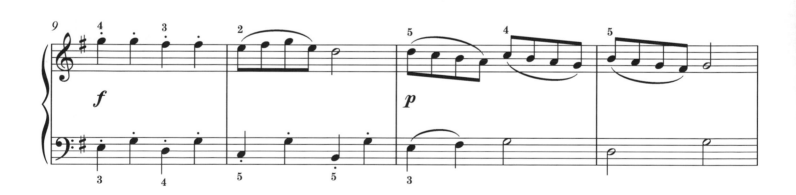

12

Fine

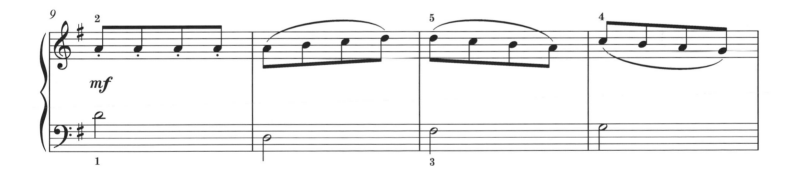

D.C. al Fine

13

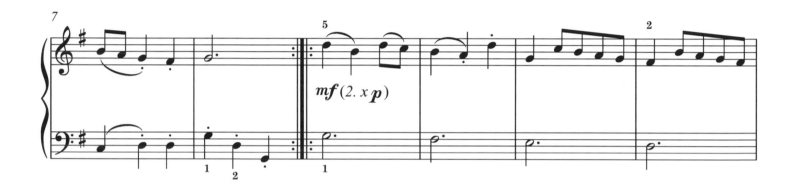

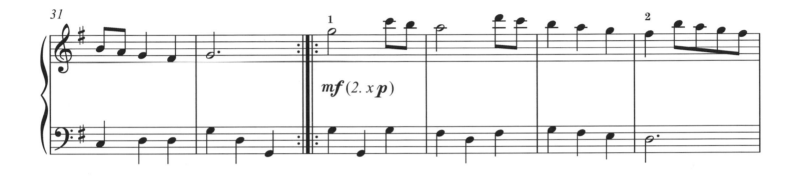

20

14

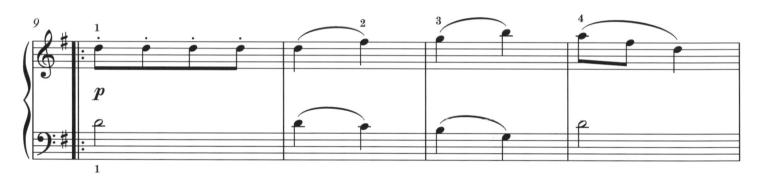

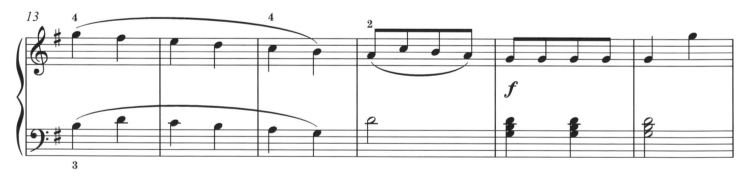

15. Andante

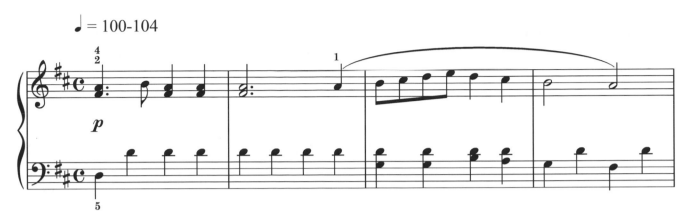

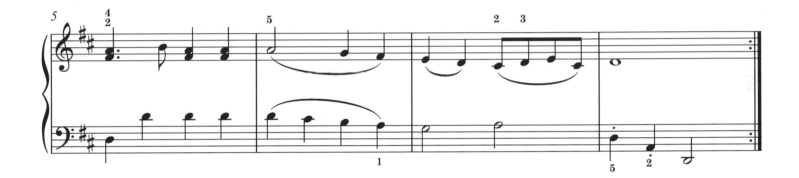

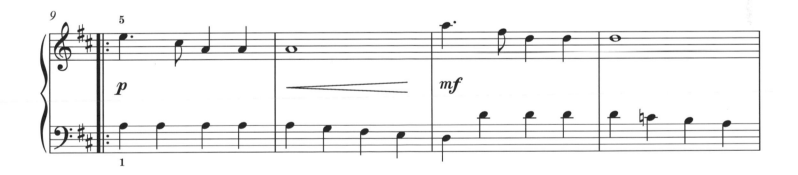

16. Minuetto

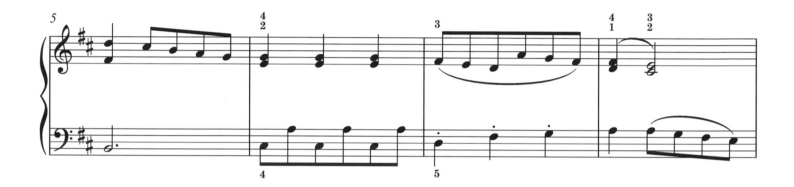

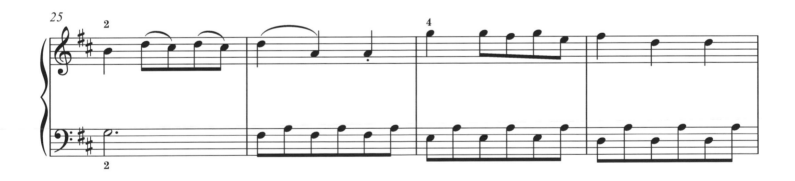

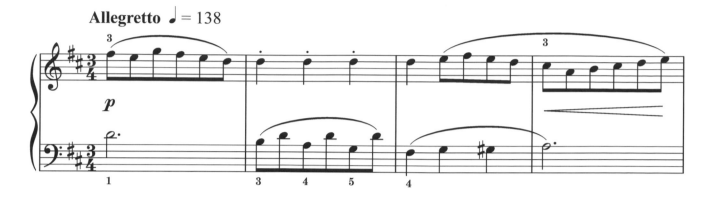

24

17. Minuetto

Allegretto ♩ = 138

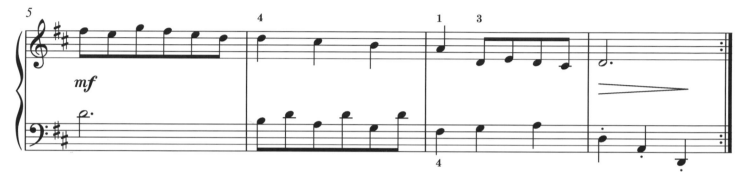

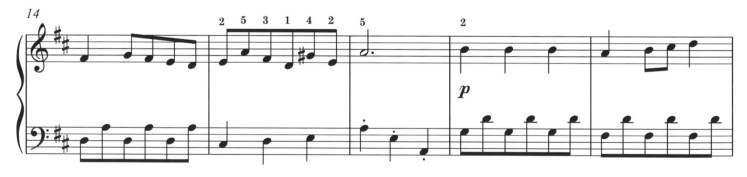

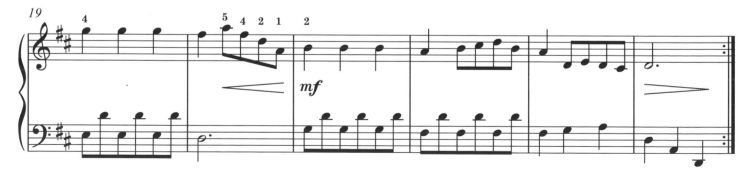

18

Allegretto ♩ = 126

19. Allegretto

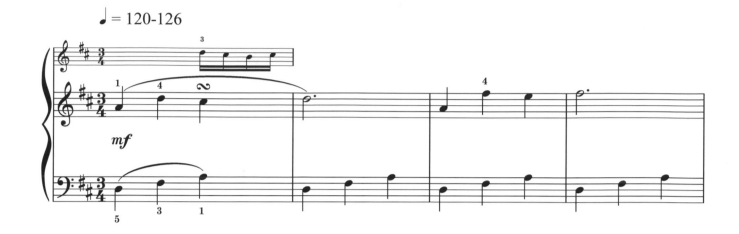

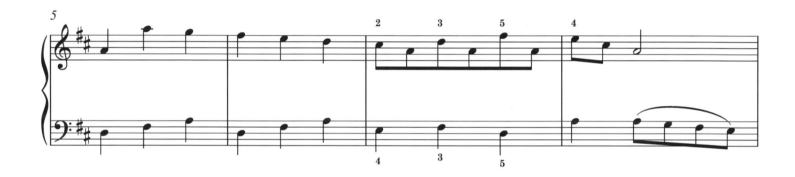

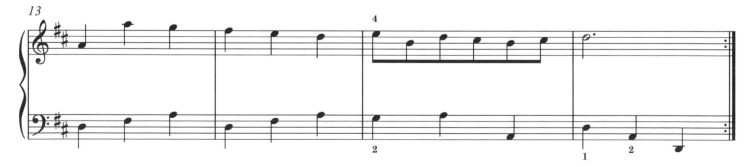

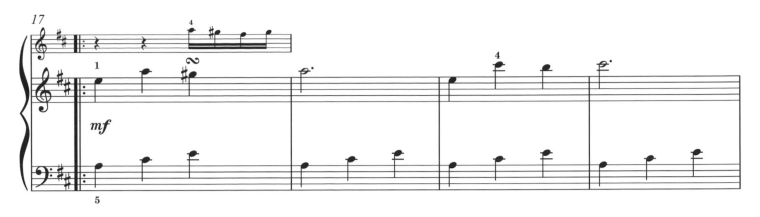

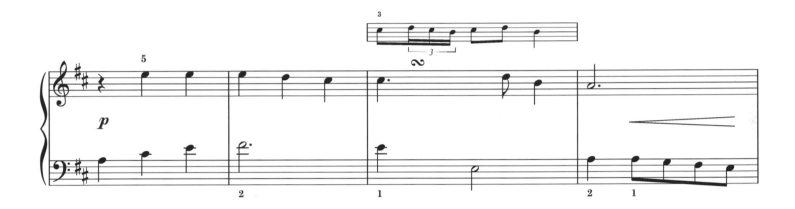

20. Presto

♩ = 160-168

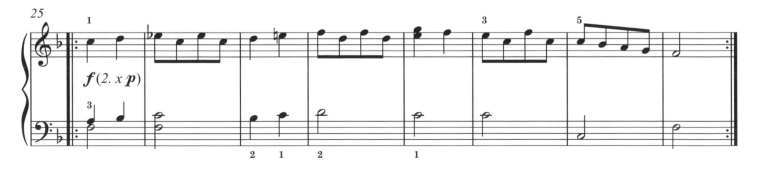

21. Allegretto

22. Andante

♩ = 108

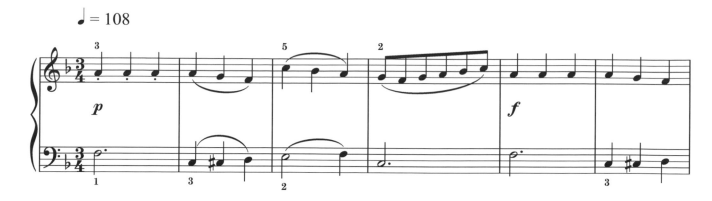

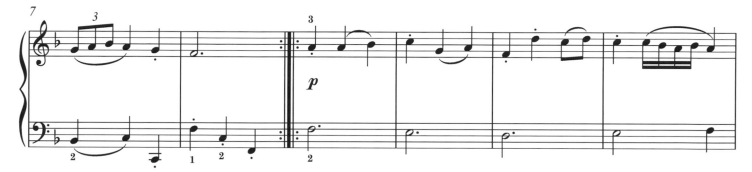

23. Allegro

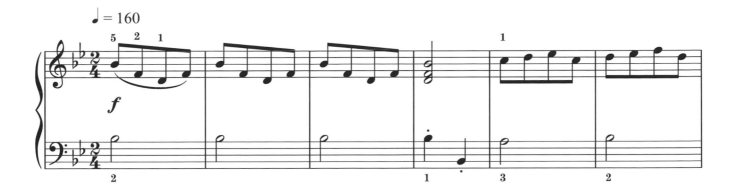

24. Allegretto

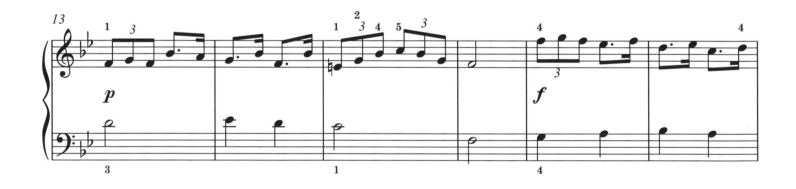